A BOOK OF THE WINTER

aug. 2 '53

The Chill of Night

A BOOK OF THE WINTER. Compiled by Edith Sitwell. New York The Vanguard Press. 114 *pp.* $3.

By Louis Untermeyer

MOST anthologies are, in the strictest sense of the phrase, readers' digests. They are usually compiled from other compilations, a culling and a condensation of six or eight already existing treasuries. Occasionally, however, an anthology appears which reveals that the compiler, ignoring the compendiums, has gone to the prime source and has so treasured the originals that the result is, in itself, a personal and original work.

Such a collection is Edith Sitwell's "A Book of the Winter." It is as keen and frosty-fresh as the season it depicts. It sparkles not only in character but in content, and even more in the way the content has been presented. Miss Sitwell declares frankly that she is not trying to make a hodgepodge of everything that has been written about winter. "In this book I have been concerned, principally, with the making of a pattern," she says, "a pattern like that, perhaps of those traceries—frost upon the windowpane, echoing the patterns of fern, of flower, of feather—which were my earliest memory." It is obvious, not only from this volume but Miss Sitwell's own poetry, that her memory is as unique as it is vivid. Here is a fantasy from the Chinese (second century B.C.) juxtaposed with fragments of John Dryden and John Donne; here are English ecstasies as traditional as rare fifteenth-century carols and as experimental as Gerard Manley Hopkins's dirge; pages as amusing as the glorification of the cat from Christopher Smart's wildly cumulative "Rejoice in the Lamb" and as exalted as "The Divine Darkness," by Dionysius the Areopagite. The book would not be Miss Sitwell's without touches of the quaint and macabre—including one delightful apparition that disappeared "with a curious perfume and most melodious twang"—as well as occasional angels among the devils.

No anthology can satisfy every reader—particularly when one reader is another anthologist—but even the least critical reader will be justified in a bit of carping. For one thing he has a right to complain of certain editorial inconsistencies. Miss Sitwell seems determined to print her French selections in the original language, but she changes her mind. Although Rimbaud, for example, appears on pages 37-8 in his native tongue, he appears on pages 77 and 113-14 in straightforward English versions. But this is a small quibble. The reader—every reader—must be grateful to Miss Sitwell for her special skill and taste, if only for including her own sprightly and lightly Skeltonian "Narrative of the Demon of Tedworth." Here is a wonderland which will, perhaps, be appreciated most in summer.

A BOOK OF THE WINTER

Compiled by

EDITH SITWELL

LONDON
MACMILLAN & CO. LTD
1950

PRINTED IN GREAT BRITAIN

TO

ALICE BOUVERIE

ACKNOWLEDGEMENTS

I OWE a deep debt of gratitude to those authors, translators and publishers who have so kindly allowed me to reproduce copyright poems and prose in this volume.

My thanks are due to Messrs. Steed and Ward, Monsieur Béguin and Miss Edith Riley, and to the executors of Monsieur Léon Bloy for their permission to include two passages from Monsieur Bloy, in the book about him written by Monsieur Béguin and translated by Miss Riley; to Mr. David Gascoyne and *Poetry London* for "Lachrymae"; to the Oxford University Press and the executors of the late Gerard Manley Hopkins for the passage from "That Nature is a Heraclitean Fire and of the Comfort of the Resurrection"; to Sir Osbert Sitwell and Messrs. Macmillan for a passage from *Escape with Me*; to Mr. John Lehmann for a passage from my novel *I Live Under a Black Sun*; to Dr. Arthur Waley and Messrs. Allen & Unwin for their kindness in allowing me to include the passage from Lady Murasaki's *The Tale of Genji* and *Blue Trousers*, and the poems from *Chinese Poems*, all these translated by Dr. Waley; to Messrs. Jonathan Cape and Mr. W. Force Stead for "The Cat" from *Rejoice with the Lamb*, by Christopher Smart; and to Mr. José Garcia Villa and the Viking Press for the poem from *Have Come, am Here.*

If by any unfortunate chance I have omitted thanks to those to whom these are due, it is by inadvertence, and I beg to offer my sincere apologies.

CONTENTS

TWO HYMNS TO THE BLESSED VIRGIN

IN THE CITY

The Godless Month

It was during the Godless Month, on a beautiful winter night, as I was leaving the Palace I saw a certain young courtier, who, when I told him I was driving out to spend the night at the Dainagans, said that my way was his and joined me. The road passed my lady's house and here it was that he alighted, saying that he had an engagement which he should have been sorry not to fulfil. The wall was half in ruins and through the gap I saw the shadowy waters of the lake. It would not have been easy (for even the moonbeams seemed to loiter here !) to hasten past so lovely a place, and when he left his coach, I left mine.

At once this man (whom I now knew to be that other lover whose existence I had guessed) went and sat unconcernedly on the bamboo sheeting and began to gaze at the moon. The chrysanthemums were just in full bloom, the bright fallen leaves were trembling and falling in the wind. It was indeed a scene of wonderful beauty that met our eyes. Presently he took a flute out of the folds of his dress, and began to play upon it. Then putting the flute aside, he began to murmur " Sweet is the shade " and other catches. Soon a pleasant-sounding native zithern began to tune up somewhere within the house and an ingenuous accompaniment was fitted to his careless warblings. Her zither was tuned to the autumn-mode, and she played with so much tenderness and feeling that though the music came from behind closed shutters it sounded quite modern and passionate, and well accorded with the soft beauty of the moonlight.

The courtier was ravished, and as he stepped forward to place himself right under her window, he turned to me and remarked in a self-satisfied voice, that among the fallen leaves no other footsteps had left its mark. Then plucking a chrysanthemum he sang

> " Strange that the music of your lute,
> These matchless flowers and all the
> beauty of the night
> Have lured no other feet to linger at
> your door."

The Tale of Genji, by Lady Murasaki.
Translated from the Japanese by Arthur Waley.

The Treasures

Hast thou entered into the treasures of the snow? or hast thou seen the treasures of the hail,

Which I have reserved against the time of trouble, against the day of battle and war?

By what way is the light parted, which scattereth the east wind upon the earth?

Who hath divided a water-course for the overflowing of waters, or a way for the lightning of thunder;

To cause it to rain on the earth, where no man is; on the wilderness, wherein there is no man;

To satisfy the desolate and waste ground; and to cause the bud of the tender herb to spring forth?

Hath the rain a father? or who hath begotten the drops of dew?

Out of whose womb came the ice? and the hoary frost of heaven, who hath gendered it?

The waters are hid as with a stone, and the face of the deep is frozen.

Canst thou bind the sweet influences of Pleiades, or loose the bands of Orion?

Canst thou bring forth Mazzaroth in his season? or canst thou guide Arcturus with his sons?

The Book of Job.

Li Fu-Jën

The sound of her silk skirt has stopped.
On the marble pavement dust grows.
The empty room is cold and still.
Fallen leaves are piled against the doors.
Longing for that lovely lady
How can I bring my aching heart to rest?

EMPEROR WU-TI (157–87).
Translated from the Chinese by Arthur Waley.

Winter Night

My bed is so empty that I keep on waking up;
As the cold increases, the night wind begins to blow.
It rustles those curtains, making a noise like the sea.
Oh that those were waves which could carry me back
to you.

EMPEROR CHIEN WÊN-TI (6th century).
Translated from the Chinese by Arthur Waley.

Time's Whiter Series

. . . . .

And now time's whiter Series is begun
Which in soft Centuries shall smoothly run.

. . . . .

JOHN DRYDEN, *Astraea Redux.*

My Love is Slaine

. . . oh, oh,
Nurse, ô my love is slaine, I saw him goe
O'er the white Alpes alone. . . .

JOHN DONNE, *Elegie XVI. On his Mistris.*

On Sailing into the Ice

I sayled not without great fear into the Ice, and I observed that the Ice was violently cast against the Rockes by force of the winds, and so made a mournfull sound afarre off, as if miserable *howlings* were heard there. Hereupon the Islanders thinke the soules of the damned are tormented in this Ice.

DITHMAR BLEFKINS, *Purchas his Pilgrimes*, XIII.

The Double Rock

Since thou hast viewed some Gorgon, and art grown
A solid stone :
To bring again to softness thy hard heart
Is past my art.
Ice may relent to water in a thaw ;
But stone made flesh Love's Chymistry ne're saw.

Therefore, by thinking on thy hardness, I
Will petrify ;
And so within our double Quarrye's Wombe,
Dig our Love's Tombe.

Thus strangely will our differences agree ;
And, with our selves, amaze the world, to see
How both Revenge and Sympathy consent
To make two Rocks each other's Monument.

HENRY KING (1592–1669).

To His Lute

My Lute awake ! perfourme the last
Labor that thou and I shall wast,
And end that I have now begon ;
For when this song is song and past,
My lute, be still, for I have done.

As to be herd where ere is none,
As lede to grave in marbill stone,
My song may perse her hert as songe :
Should we then sing, or sigh, or mone ?
No ! no ! my lute ! for I have done.

The Rokkes do not so cruelly
Repulse the waves continually
As she my suyte, and affection ;
So that I am past remedy,
Whereby my lute and I have done.

. . . . .

Vengeance shall fall on thy disdaine
That makest but game of ernest pain ;
Thinck not alone under the sonne
Unquyt to cause thy lovers playn,
All tho my lute and I have done.

Perchaunce the lye wethered and old
The winter nyghts that are so cold
Playning in vain unto the moone ;
Thy wishes then dare not be told ;
Care then who lyst, for I have done.

And then may chaunce the to repent
The tyme that thou hast lost and spent
To cause thy lovers sigh and swone,
Then shalt thou know beaultie but lent,
And wisshe and want as I have done.

Now cease, my lute : this is the last
Labor that thou and I shalt wast,
And ended is that we begon :
Now is this song both song and past,
My lute be still, for I have done.

SIR THOMAS WYATT.

Sonnet

Innumerable Beauties, thou white haire
Spredde forth like to a Region of the Aire,
Curl'd like a sea, and like Etheriall fire
Dost from thy vitall principles aspire
To bee the highest Element of faire,
From thy proud heights, thou so commandst desire
That when it would presume, it grows, dispare,
And from it selfe a Vengeance doth require,
While absolute in that thy braue command
Knittinge each haire, into an awfull frowne

Like to an Hoste of Lightninges, thou dost stand
To ruine all that fall not prostrate downe ;
While to the humble like a beamy Crowne
Thou seemest wreathed, by some immortall Hande.

LORD HERBERT OF CHERBURY.

The Northern Lights

I do not remember to have met with any travellers into high Northern latitudes, who remarked their having heard the Northern Lights make any noise in the air as they vary their colours or position ; which may probably be owing to the want of perfect silence at the time they made their observations on these meteors. I can positively affirm, that on still nights I have heard them make a rustling and crackling noise like the waving of a large flag in a fresh gale of wind.

SAMUEL HEARNE, *Journey from Prince of Wales Fort in Hudson Bay to the Northern Ocean*, 1795.

Meteors

It were endless to mention all the different Figures these Meteors put on, and the different Motions wherewith they are agitated. Their motion is most commonly like that of a pair of Colours waved in the Air and the different Tints of the Light give them the appearance of so many Streamers of that sort of Taffetas which we call changeable. Sometimes they line a part of the sky with scarlet. On the 15th of December I saw at Oswer-

Tornea a Phenomenon of this kind, which raised my admiration, in the midst of all the Wonders. I was now every day accustomed to it. There appeared to the South, a great space of the sky tinged with so lively a red, that the whole Constellation of Orion look'd as if it had been dipt in blood. This Light, which was fixt at first, soon moved, and changing to other colours, Violet and Blue, settled into a Dome, whose top stood a little to the South and West of the Zenith. The Moon shone bright, but did not in the least efface it. In this country, where there are Lights of many different colours, I never saw but two that were red; and such are taken as Presages of a great Misfortune.

MAUPERTIUS, *The Figure of the Earth.* Determined from observations made by Order of the French King at the Polar Circle, 1736.

Winter Morning

This was the morning when, with Her, you struggled among those banks of snow, those green-lipped crevasses, that ice, those black flags and blue rays, and the purple perfumes of the polar sun.

ARTHUR RIMBAUD, "Metropolitan."
Translated from the French by Helen Rootham.

Winter Sunset: Winter Dawn

. . . the starry meadows beyond Orion, where, for pansies and violets, and heart-ease, are the beds of the triplicate and many-tinted Suns.

EDGAR ALLAN POE, *The Power of Words.*

The Seasons Alter

. . . . .

The seasons alter : hoary-headed frosts
Fall in the fresh lap of the crimson rose,
And on old Hyem's thin and icie crowne
An odorous Chaplet of sweet sommer buds
Is, as in mockery, set.

WILLIAM SHAKESPEARE,
A Midsommer Night's Dreame, Act II, Scene I.

The Sick Rose

O Rose, thou art sick !
The invisible worm
That flies in the night
In the howling storm

Has found out thy bed
Of crimson joy,
And his dark secret love
Does thy life destroy.

WILLIAM BLAKE.

Winter the Huntsman

Through his iron glades
Rides Winter the Huntsman.
All colour fades
As his horn is heard sighing.

Far through the forest
His wild hooves crash and thunder
Till many a mighty branch
Is torn asunder.

As night creeps from the ground,
Hides each tree from its brother,
And each dying sound
Reveals yet another.

Is it Winter the Huntsman
Who gallops through his iron glades,
Cracking his cruel whip
To the gathering shades?

OSBERT SITWELL.

Of the Winter Earth

Seeds themselves do lye in perpetual shades. . . . Darknesse and Light hold interchangeable dominions, and alternately rule the seminal state of things. Light unto Pluto is darknesse unto Jupiter. Legions of seminal Ideas lye in their second Chaos and Orcus of Hippocrates.

SIR THOMAS BROWNE, *The Garden of Cyrus.*

Our Longest Sun

. . . Our longest sun sets at right descensions, and makes but winter arches, and therefore it cannot be long before we lye down in darknesse.

SIR THOMAS BROWNE, *Urn Burial.*

Games

The ordinary recreations which we have in Winter, and in most solitarie times busie our minds with, as Cards, Tables, and Dice, Shovel-board, Chesse-play . . . Shuttlecock, billiards, musicke, masks, singing, dancing, ale-games, frolicks, jests, riddles, catches, purposes, questions and commands, merry tales of errant Knights, Queens, Lovers, Lords, Ladies, Giants, Dwarfs, Thieves, Cheaters, Witches, Fayries, Goblins, Friers, etc. . . . And the rest, which some delight to heare, some to tell, and all are well pleased with.

ROBERT BURTON, *The Anatomy of Melancholy.*

With Feather Litter of the Cold

. . . .

The Courts with feather litter of the cold are filled
And the dead woods hear no hunting horn.

SACHEVERELL SITWELL, *Doctor Donne and Gargantua.*

So, we'll go no more a-roving

So, we'll go no more a-roving
So late into the night,
Though the heart be still as loving,
And the moon be still as bright.

For the sword outwears its sheath,
And the soul wears out the breast,
And the heart must pause to breathe,
And love itself have rest.

Though the night was made for loving,
And the day returns too soon,
Yet we'll go no more a-roving
By the light of the moon.

LORD BYRON.

Of the Snow

Out of these small vaporous drops the snow is first generated. First of all, you see a small drop, as big as a single sand. This is augmented or increased by the fog. . . . Then it freezes and splits asunder, so that you see the figure of a star, which yet is still frozen together, until in time it is quite pointed or divided asunder one from the other; and then you see a star with six points, which points are not yet quite frozen, because there are still hanging some wet drops between the points, until it at length assumes the perfect form of a star, with points serrated at the sides, like ferns, on the points whereof still hang some drops . . . which are lost at last, and so it is turned into an exact and perfect star, which is seen in the severest frosts so long until it loseth all its points. As to the many sorts of snow . . . I have made these following observations and distinctions. . . . The snow that falleth where it is tolerably cold and rainy withall . . . falls like unto small roses, needles, and small corns: when the cold weather doth remit, the snow falleth like stars, with many points, like the leaves of ferne. . . . When it is very cold, but not windy withal, the snow falleth like stars, in a cluster because the wind cannot blow them asunder.

F. MARTENS, *Voyage to Spitzbergen.*

D'Anne qui luy jecta de la neige

Anne par jeu me jecta de la neige
Que je cuidoys froide certainement
Mais c'estoit feu. L'expérience en ay-je
Car embrasé je fuz certainement.
Dedans, la neige ni trouverai-je place
Pour l'ardre point ? Anne, ta seule grâce
Estaindre peult le feu que je sens bien
Non point par eau, par neige, ni par glace,
Mais par sentir ung feu pareil au mien.

CLÉMENT MAROT.

The White Light

I

Une lumière éclatante de blancheur, répandue autour de mes épaules, me vêt tout le corps de ses purs rayons : et cette lumière-là n'est pas du tout semblable à la sombre lumière qui, mélangée d'ombre, obscurent nos regards : sa céleste origine n'a rien de la lumière terrestre. Une divinité insinue dans ma poitrine je ne sais quoi de céleste qui coule en moi comme à plein flot.

ARTHUR RIMBAUD, aetat. 14.

II

C'est un éclat qui n'éblouit point, c'est une blancheur suave, une splendeur infuse, qui charme délicieusement la vue sans la fatiguer. Quant à la clarté à l'aide de laquelle on perçoit cette beauté divine, c'est une lumière entièrement différente de celle d'ici-bas. La clarté du soleil semble même si terne en comparaison de cet éclat, de cette splendeur qui s'offre à nos regards intérieurs, qu'on voudrait ensuite ne plus ouvrir les yeux.

SAINTE THÉRÈSE D'AVILA.

Le vierge, le vivace, et le bel aujourd'hui

Le vierge, le vivace et le bel aujourd'hui
Va-t-il nous déchirer avec un coup d'aile ivre
Ce lac dur oublié que hante sous le givre
Le transparent glacier des vols qui n'ont pas fui !

Un cygne d'autrefois se souvient que c'est lui,
Magnifique mais qui sans espoir se délivre
Pour n'avoir pas chanté la région où vivre
Quand du stérile hiver a resplendi l'ennui.

Tout son col secouera cette blanche agonie
Par l'espace infligée à l'oiseau qui le nie,
Mais non l'horreur du sol où le plumage est pris.

Fantôme qu'à ce lieu son pur éclat assigne,
Il s'immobilise au songe froid de mépris
Que vêt parmi l'exil inutile le Cygne.

STÉPHANE MALLARMÉ.

Soft Snow

I walked abroad on a snowy day :
I ask'd the soft snow with me to play :
She play'd and she melted in all her prime,
And the winter call'd it a dreadful crime.

WILLIAM BLAKE.

Blacke is the beauty of the brightest day

Blacke is the beauty of the brightest day,
The golden balle of heauen's eternal fire,
That danc'd with glorie on the siluer waues :
Now wants the fewell that enflamde his beames
And all with faintnesse and for foule disgrace,
He bindes his temples with a frowning cloude,
Ready to darken earth with endlesse night :
Zenocrate that gaue him light and life,
Whose eies shot fire from their Iuory bowers,
And tempered euery soule with liuely heat,
Now by the malice of the angry Skies,
Whose icalousie admits no second Mate,
Drawes in the comfort of her latest breath
All dasled with the hellish mists of death.
Now walk the angels on the walles of heauen,
As Centinels to warne th' immortall soules,
To entertaine deuine *Zenocrate*.
Apollo, *Cynthia*, and the ceaselesse lamps
That gently look'd vpon this loathsome earth,
Shine downwards now no more, but deck the heauens
To entertaine diuine *Zenocrate*.
The chrystall springs whose taste illuminates
Refined eies with an eternall sight,
Like tried siluer runs through Paradice
To entertaine diuine *Zenocrate*.
The Cherubins and holy Seraphins
That sing and play before the King of Kings,
Vse all their voices and their instruments
To entertaine diuine *Zenocrate*.

CHRISTOPHER MARLOWE,
Tamburlaine, Act 2, Scaena ultima.

FOR CHRISTMAS DAY

I

Of Christ and the Rose

Rosa passionis effusionibus crebris sacratissimi sanguinis sui specialiter fuit rubricata.

(The effusion of His Sacred Blood has reddened the leaves of the Rose, bleeding for His Sufferings.)

St. Bernard, Opera 8.

II

My most. My most. O my lost!

My most. My most. O my lost!
O my bright, my ineradicable ghost.
At whose bright coast God seeks
Shelter and is lost is lost. O
Coast of Brightness. O cause of
Grief. O rose of purest grief.
O thou in my breast so stark and
Holy-bright. O thou melancholy
Light. Me. Me. My own perfidy.
O my most my most. O the bright
The beautiful, the terrible Accost.

José Garcia Villa.

III

The Burning Babe

As I in hoary winter's night
  Stood shivering in the snow,

Surprised I was with sudden heat
  Which made my heart to glow ;
And lifting up a fearful eye
  To view what fire was near,
A pretty babe all burning bright
  Did in the air appear.
Who, scorchèd with excessive heat,
  Such floods of tears did shed,
As though His floods should quench His flames
  Which, with His tears, were bred :
" Alas ! " quoth He, " but newly born
  In fiery heats I fry,
Yet none approach to warm their hearts
  Or feel my fire but I.

" My faultless breast the furnace is,
  The fuel, wounding thorns ;
Love is the fire, and sighs the smoke,
  The ashes, shames and scorns ;
The fuel Justice layeth on,
  And Mercy blows the coals,
The metal in this furnace wrought
  Are men's defilèd souls :
For which, as now on fire I am
  To work them to my good,
So will I melt into a bath
  To wash them in my blood."
With this He vanished out of sight
  And swiftly shrunk away,
And straight I called into my mind
  That it was Christmas Day.

ROBERT SOUTHWELL, *Martyr.*

IV

Ah my dere

" Ah my dere, ah my dere Son,"
  Said Mary, " ah my dere,
Kiss thy mother, Jesu,
  With a laughing chere."

This enders night
I saw a sight
  All in my slepe ;
Mary, that may,
She sang " Lullay "
  And sore did weep.

To kepe she soght
Full fast about
  Her son fro colde.
Joseph said " Wyfe,
My joy, my lyfe,
  Say what ye wolde."

" No thing, my spouse,
Is in this house,
  Unto my pay ;
My son, a kyng,
That made all thyng,
  Lyeth in hay."

" My mother dere
Amend your chere
  And now be still ;
Thus for to lye
It is soothly
  My Father's will.

Derisyon,
Great passyon.
  Infinitely,
As it is found,
Many a wound
  Suffer shall I.

On Calvary
That is so hye,
  There shall I be,
Man to restore,
Naylit full sore
  Upon a tree."

ANON. (15th century).

V

I sing of a maiden

I sing of a maiden
  That is makeles,
King of all Kings
  To her son she ches.

He came al so stille
  Ther his moder was,
As dew in Aprille
  That falleth on the grass.

He came al so stille
  To his moder's bour,
As dew in Aprille
  That falleth on the flour.

He came al so stille,
  Ther his moder lay
As dew in Aprille
  That falleth on the spray.

Moder and maiden
  Was never non but sche ;
Well may such a lady
  Gode's moder be.

ANON. (15th century).

VI

Adam lay i-bowyndyn

Adam lay i-bowyndyn,
  bowyndyn in a bond—
foure thousand wynter
  thoght he not too long ;
And al was for an appil,
  An appil that he tok,
As clerkés fyndyn
  Writen in here book—
Ne hadde the appil takë ben,
  the appil taken ben,
Ne haddë never our lady
  A ben hevenë quene.
blyssid be the tyme
  that appil takë was.
ther fore we mown syngyn
  Deo gracias.

ANON. (15th century).

VII

Haylle, comely and clene

PRIMUS PASTOR

Haylle, comely and clene :
Haylle, young child.
Haylle, maker, as I mene
Of a maidyn so mylde.
Thou hast waryd, I weyne,
The warlo so wylde,
The fals gyler of teyn,
Now goys he begylde.
    Lo, he merys,
Lo, he laughes, my swetyng,
A wel fare metyng,
I have holden my hetyng,
    Have a bob of cherys.

SECUNDUS PASTOR

Haylle, sufferan Savyoure,
For thou hast us soght :
Haylle, frely foyde and floure
That all things hath wroght.
Haylle, full of favoure,
That made alle of noght.
Haylle, I kneyle and I cowre.
A byrd have I broght
    To my barne.
Haylle, lytylle tinë mop,
Of our crede thou art crop :
I wold drynk on thy cop.
Lytylle day starre.

TERTIUS PASTOR

Haylle, derlyng dere,
Fulle of Godhede,
I pray the be nere
When that I have nede.
Haylle, swete is thy chere :
My hart wold blede
To see the sytt here
In so poorë wede
    With no penys.
Haylle ! put forth thy dalle.
I bring the bat a balle
Have and play the with-alle
    And go to the tenys.

ANON. (15th century). The Towneley MSS.

GLOSSARY.—*waryd :* cursed. *warlo :* wizard. *gyler :* beguiler. *teyn :* evil. *goys :* goes. *merys :* merry is. *hetyng :* promise. *frely foyde :* noble child. *crop :* head. *cop :* cup. *dalle :* hand. *tenys :* tennis.

VIII

Veni, Coronaberis

Surge mea sponsa, swete in sight,
And se thi sone thou gafe souke so scheene ;
Thou schalt abide with thi babe so bright,
And in my glorie be callide a queene.
Thi mammilis, moder, ful well y meane,
Y had to my meete that y myght not mys ;
Above all creatures, my moder clene,
Veni, coronaberis.

Come, clenner than cristal, to my cage ;
Columba mea, y thee calle,

And se thi sone that in seruage
For manny's soule was made a thralle.
In this paliys so principal
I pleyde priuyli withoute mys,
Myn high cage, moder, have thou schal;
Veni, coronaberis.

For macula, moder, was nevere in thee:
Filia syon, thou art the flour;
Ful sweteli shalt thou sitte bi me,
And bear a crowne with me in tour,
And alle my seintis to thin honour
Schal honoure thee, moder, in my blis,
That blessid bodi that bare me in bowur:
Veni, coronaberis.

Tota pulchra thou art to my plesynge,
My moder, princes of paradiys,
Of the a watir ful well gan sprynge
That schal agen all my rightis rise;
The welle of mercy in thee, moder, liys
To bringe thi blessid bodi to blis;
And my seintis schulen do thee service,
Veni, coronaberis.

Veni, electa mea, my moder swete,
Whanne thou bad me, babe, be full stille,
Ful godli oure lippis than gan mete,
With bright braunchis as blosmes on hills.
Favus distillans it wente with wille,
Out of our lippis whanne we did kis,
Therfor, moder, now, ful stille,
Veni, coronaberis.

Veni de libano, thou loneli in launche,
That lappid me loueli with liking song,
Thou schalt abide with a blessid braunche,
That so semeli of thi bodi sprong.
Ego, flos campi, thi flour, was solde,
That on Calueri to thee cried y-wys,
Moder, thou woost this as y wolde ;
Veni, coronaberis.

Pulcra vt luna, thou berist the lamme,
As the sunne that schinest clere,
Veni in ortum meum, thou deintiest damme,
To smelle my spices that here ben in fere.
My paliys is pight for thi pleasure,
Ful of bright braunches and blosmes of blis ;
Come now, moder, to thi derling dere.
Veni, coronaberis.

Quid est ista, so vertuose,
That is evere lastyng for hir mekenes ?
Aurora consurgens graciouse,
So benigne a ladi, of rich brightnes,
This is the colour of kinde clennes,
Regina celi, that neuere dide mys ;
Thus endeth the song of great sweettness,
Veni, coronaberis.

Lambeth MS. (*c.* 1430).

GLOSSARY.—*scheene :* shine. *mammilis :* breasts. *seruage :* servitude. *paliys :* palace. *mys :* amiss. *watir ful well :* well filled with water. *schulen :* shall. *lamme :* light. *fere :* crowd.

IX

Of a rose, a lovely rose

Of a rose, a lovely rose,
Of a rose is al myn song.

Lestynt, lordynges, both elde and ynge,
How this rosë began to sprynge ;
Swych a rosë to myn lykynge
In all this world ne knowe I non.

The aungil cam fro hevenë tour,
To grete Marye with gret honour,
And seidë sche schuld bere the flour,
That schuldë breke the fendës bond.

The flour sprong in heye Bedlem,
That is bothë bryght and schene,
The rose is Mary, hevenë quene,
Out of her bosum the blosmë sprong.

The ferstë braunche is full of might,
That sprong on Crystemesse nyght :
The sterre schon over Bedlem bryght,
That is bothë brod and long.

The second braunchë sprong to helle,
The fendës power down to felle ;
Therein myght non sowle dwelle
Blessed be the tyme the rose sprong.

The threddë braunche is good and swote,
It sprong to hevenë crop and rote,
Therein to dwelle and ben our bote ;
Every day it schewit in prestes hand.

Prey we to here with gret honour,
Sche that bare the blessid flour,
Sche be our helpe and our socour,
And schild us fro the fendës hand.

ANON.

X

Al the meryere

Al the meryere is that place
the sunne of grace hym schynit in.

The sunne of grace hym schynit in
  in on day quan it was morwe
quan our Lord God born was
  withoute wem or sorwe

The sunne of grace hym schynit in
  on a day quan it was pryme
quan our Lord God born was
  so wel he knew his tyme

The sunne of grace hym schynit in
  on a day quan it was non
quan our Lord God born was
  And on the rode don

The sunne of grace hym schynit in
  on a day quan it was undyrn
quan our Lord God born was
  and to the herte stongyn.

ANON.

GLOSSARY.—*wem* : stain. *quan* : when. *undyrn* : morning. *stongyn* : stung.

TWO HYMNS TO THE BLESSED VIRGIN

I

O Mooder Mayde

O mooder Mayde ! O mayde Mooder free !
O bussh unbrent, brennynge in Moyses' sighte,
That ravyshedest doun fro the Deitee,
Thurgh thyn humblesse, the Goost that in th' alighte
Of whos vertu, whan he thyn herte lighte,
Conceyved was the Fadre's sapience,
Help me to telle it in thy reverence.

Lady, thy bountee, thy magnificence,
Thy vertu, and thy grete humylitee,
Ther may no tonge expresse in no science ;
For somtyme, Lady, er men praye to thee,
Thou goost biforn of thy benignytee
And getest us the lyght thurgh thy preyere
To gyden us unto thy Sone so deere.

GEOFFREY CHAUCER, Prologue to *The Prioress's Tale.*

II

Ballade que Villon feit à la requeste de sa mère pour prier Nostre Dame

Dame des cieulx, régente terrienne,
Empérieure des inferneaux palus,
Recevez-moi, vostre humble chrestienne,
Que comprense soy, entre vos esleuz.

Ce non obstant qu'oncques rien ne valus.
Les biens de vous, ma dame et ma maistresse
Sont trop plus grans qui ne suis pêcheresse,
Sans lesquels biens âme ne peut mérir
N'avoir les cieulx, je n'en suis jangleresse.
En ceste foi je vueil vivre et mourir.

A vostre Filz dicte que je suis sienne ;
De luy soyent mes pêchiez absolus :
Pardonne moy comme a l'Égyptienne,
Ou comme il feist au clerc Thiophilus,
Lequel par vous fut quitte et absoluz,
Combien qu'il eust au diable fait promesse.
Préservez-moy, que ne fait jamais ce,
Vierge portant, sans rompure mourir
Le sacrament qu'on célèbre à la messe.
En ceste foy je vueil vivre et mourir.

Femme je suis povrette et ancienne,
Qui rien ne sçay ; oncques lettre ne leuz ;
Au moustier voy donz suis paroissienne
Paradis peint, où sont harpes et luz,
Et, ung enfer où dampnez sont boulluz.
L'ung me fait paour, l'autre joye et liesse.
La joye avoir my fay, haute Déesse,
Ce qui pêcheurs doivent nous recourir,
Combien de foy, sans faute ni paresse,
En ceste foy je vueil vivre et mourir.

ENVOY

Vous portastes, digne Vierge, princesse,
Jésus régnant, qui n'a fin de cesse.
Tout-Puissant, prenant nostre foiblesse,

Laissez les cieulx et nous vint sécourir,
Offrit à mort sa très chère jeunesse.
Nostre Seigneur tel est, tel le confesse,
En ceste foy je vueil vivre et mourir.

François Villon.

A Litany

Drop, drop, slow tears,
And bathe those bounteous feet
Which brought from Heaven
The news and Prince of peace :
Cease not, wet eyes
His mercy to intreat ;
To crie for vengeance
Sinne doth never cease :
In your deep floods
Drown all my faults and fears,
Nor let his eye
See sinne, but through my tears.

Phineas Fletcher.

Lachrymae

Slow are the years of light :
And more immense
Than the imagination. And the years return
Until the Unity is filled. And heavy are
The lengths of Time with the slow weight of tears.
Since thou didst weep, on a remote hill-side
Beneath the olive-trees, fires of unnumbered stars
Have burnt the years away, until we see them now :

Since Thou didst weep, as many tears
Have flowed like hourglass sand.
Thy tears were all.
And when our secret face
Is blind because of the mysterious
Surging of tears wrung by our most profound
Presentiment of evil in man's fate, our cruellest wounds
Become Thy stigmata. They are Thy tears which fall.

DAVID GASCOYNE.

Aire and Angels

Twice or thrice had I loved thee,
Before I knew thy face or name,
So in a voice, so in a shapelesse flame,
Angells affect us oft, and worship'd bee;
Still when, to where thou wert, I came,
Some lovely glorious nothing I did see.
But since my soule, whose child love is,
Takes limmes of flesh, and else could nothing doe,
More subtile than the parent is,
Love must not be, but take a body too,
And therefore what thou wert, and who,
I bid Love aske, and now
That it assume thy body, I allow,
And fixe it selfe in thy lip, eye, and brow.

Whilst thus to ballast love, I thought,
And so more steadily to have gone,
With wares which would sinke admiration,
I saw, I had love's pinnace overfraught,
Ev'ry thy haire for love to worke upon

Is much too much, some fitter must be sought ;
For, nor in nothing, nor in things
Extreme, and scatt'ring bright, can love inhere ;
Then as an Angell, face and wings
Of aire, not pure as it, yet pure doth weare,
So thy love may be my love's spheare ;
Just such disparitie
As is twixt Aire and Angells puritie
Twixt women's love, and men's will ever bee.

JOHN DONNE.

A Song from a Booke of Ayres

Followe thy faire sunne, vnhappy shadowe !
Though thou be blacke as night,
And she made all of light,
Yet follow thy faire sun, vnhappy shadowe.

Follow her whose light thy light depriueth.
Though here thou liu'st disgrac't,
And she in heauen is plac't,
Yet follow her whose light the world reuiueth.

Follow those pure beames, whose beautie burneth !
That so have scorchèd thee,
As thou still blacke must bee,
Till her kind beames thy black to brightnes turneth.

Follow her, while yet her glorie shineth.
There comes a luckles night,
That will dim all her light ;
And this the black vnhappie shade deuineth.

Follow still, since so thy fates ordainèd.
The sun must haue his shade,
Till both at once doe fade,
The Sun still proud, the shadow still disdainèd.

THOMAS CAMPION.

A Nocturnall upon S. Lucies Day: Being the Shortest Day

Tis the yeares midnight, and it is the dayes,
Lucies, who scarce seaven houres herself unmaskes,
The Sunne is spent, and now his flasks
Send forth light squibs, no constant rayes ;
The world's whole sap is sunke :
The generall balme th' hydroptique earth hath drunke.
Whither, as to the beds-feet, life is shrunke,
Dead and enterr'd ; yet all these seeme to laugh
Compar'd with mee, who am their Epitaph.

Study me then, you who shall lovers bee
At the next world, that is, at the next Spring :
For I am every dead thing,
In whom love wrought new Alchimie.
For his art did expresse
A quintessence even from nothingnesse,
From dull privations, and leane emptinesse :
He ruined mee, and I am re-begot
Of absence, darknesse, death ; things which are not.

All others, from all things, draw all that's good,
Life, soule, forme, spirit, whence they being have ;
I, by love's limbecke, am the grave
Of all, that's nothing. Oft a flood
Have wee two wept, and so

Drown'd the whole world, us two ; oft did we grow
To be two Chaosses, when we did show
Care to ought else ; and often absences
Withdrew our soules, and made us carcasses.

But I am by her death (which word wrongs her)
Of the first nothing, the Elixir grown ;
Were I a man, that I were one,
I needs must know ; I should preferre,
If I were any beast,
Some ends, some means ; Yea plants, yea stones detest,
And love ; All, all, some properties invest ;
If I an ordinary nothing were,
As shadow, a light, and body must be here.

But I am None ; nor will my Sunne renew.
You lovers, for whose sake, the lesser Sunne
At this time to the Goat is runne
To fetch new lust, and give it you,
Enjoy your summer all ;
Since shee enjoyes her long night's festivall,
Let mee prepare towards her, and let mee call
This houre her Vigill, and her Eve, since this
Both the yeares, and the dayes deep midnight is.

JOHN DONNE.

IN THE CITY

I

Les Sept Vieillards

à Victor Hugo

Fourmillante cité, cité pleine de rêves,
Où le spectre, en plein jour raccroche le passant !
Les mystères partout coulent comme des sèves
Dans les canaux étroits du colosse puissant.

Un matin, cependant que dans la triste rue
Les maisons, dont la brume allongeait la hauteur,
Simulaient les deux quais d'une rivière accrue,
Et que, décor semblable à l'âme de l'acteur,

Un brouillard sale et jaune inondait tout l'espace,
Je suivais, roidissant mes nerfs comme un héros
Et discutant avec mon âme déjà lasse,
Le faubourg secoué par les lourds tombereaux.

Tout à coup, un vieillard dont les guenilles jaunes
Imitaient la couleur de ce ciel pluvieux,
Et dont l'aspect aurait fait pleuvoir des aumônes,
Sans la méchanceté qui luisait dans les yeux,

M'apparut. On eût dit sa prunelle trempée
Dans le fiel ; son regard aiguisait le frimas,
Et sa barbe à longs poils, roide comme une épeé,
Se projetait, pareille à celle de Judas.

Il n'était pas voûté, mais cassé, son échine
Faisait avec sa jambe un parfait angle droit,
Si bien que son bâton, parachevant sa mine,
Lui donnait la tournure et le pas maladroit

D'un quadrupède infirme ou d'un juif à trois pattes.
Dans la neige et la boue il allait s'empêtrant,
Comme s'il écrasait des morts sous ses savates,
Hostile à l'univers plutôt qu'un indifférent.

Son pareil le suivait : barbe, œil, dos, bâton, loques,
Nul trait se distinguait, du même enfer venu,
Ce jumeau centenaire, et ces spectres baroques
Marchaient du même pas vers un but inconnu.

A quel complot infâme étais-je donc en butte,
Ou quel méchant hasard ainsi m'humiliait !
Car je comptai sept fois, de minute en minute,
Ce sinistre vieillard qui se multiplait !

Que celui-là qui rit de mon inquiétude,
Et qui n'est pas saisi d'un frisson fraternel,
Songe bien que malgré tant de décrépitude
Ces sept monstres hideux avaient l'air éternel.

Aurais-je, sans mourir, contemplé le huitième,
Sosie, inexorable, ironique et fatal
Dégoûtant Phénix, fils et père de lui-même ?
Mais je tournai le dos au cortège infernal.

Exaspéré comme un ivrogne qui voit double,
Je rentrai, je fermai ma porte, épouvanté,
Malade et morfondu, l'esprit fiévreux et trouble,
Blessé par le mystère et par l'absurdité.

Vainement ma raison voulait prendre la barre :
La tempête en jouant déroutait ses efforts,
Et mon âme dansait, vieille gabare
Sans mâts, sur une mer monstrueuse et sans bords.

CHARLES BAUDELAIRE.

II

Under the Fog

All through the day, under the Bedlam daylight's murderous roar, changing to the enormous Tartarean darkness of a fog, through the city's deepest circles of Hell all forms of misery loomed and faded, monstrous shapes, their sightless faces turned to the unheeding sky, tapping upon the ground with a hollow noise that seemed to echo down millions of fathoms to the very centre of the earth. For in this city of night only the blind can see.

Then the fog changed ; it was no longer a muffling deadening thickness, a world-wide chaos ; it was another form of night that had suddenly descended upon the city, black, appallingly clear, and cold as the blackness of Hell's day. And in this darkness the palaces seemed even more world-high ; the enormous city seemed of black marble and basalt, and even the trees were changed to this.

Sometimes an elegant figure would shine through the night, circling swiftly as if it were a swallow, or floating, a black swan, on the wide water-black marble pavements ; and a faint perfume would fall like the first faint flakes of snow. But these beings came from another world, from a universe where there are water-falls of satin and of velvet, where there are fires like the Midnight Sun. Their faces Chinese from the cold, high-cheek-boned, ancient and mysterious, these beings passed by, circling like swallows, floating like black swans,—or alighted from motors and stepped into the shops.

Then the universe of beggars rushed towards them, a sea of rags fluttered about them ; as the carriages stopped beside the shops, so brightly lighted in the blackness that the windows seemed fountains of jewels, the beggars, their shapes made monstrous by the changing darkness, huge and menacing, appeared from all sides. "These," wrote the man under the black sun,[1] "watching their opportunity, crowded to the sides of the coach, and gave one the most horrible spectacles that ever an European eye beheld."

One woman had a disease, into the wounds of which, into whose unutterable misery "I could easily have crept and covered my whole body." There, in that lulling maternity, whose disease is the symbol of the horror into which we have deformed Nature, one could seek a refuge, even as we creep into the wounds, the diseases of civilisation, and lie at ease there. In the gigantic fog, the shapes of all men were changed, misery loomed larger. "There was a fellow with a wen on his neck, larger than five wool-packs, and another with a couple of wooden legs, each about twenty foot high. But the most hateful sight of all was the lice crawling on their clothes ; I could see distinctly the limbs of these vermin with my naked eye. . . . And their snouts with which they rooted like swine."

In the centre of the city, near the enormous lumbering palaces of commerce, little smooth people were running to and fro from the Exchange, running or walking slowly.

[1] Jonathan Swift.

But it was in the fashionable quarters, along the wide pavements that were cold and hard as Hell's huge polar street, cold as the universal blackness of Hell's day, that the fluttering towers of rags and bones were swept — each a universe of misery, a world of hunger and polar wastes, shut off from all others. Some were young, and these had nothing between their one outer covering of rags and their skin, so that it seemed they had early been made ready for the grave. With those who were older, it was as if all the nations of the dead with their million-year-old rags about them, had risen to denounce us. They had no identity, their faces were extinct. They would have been sexless as the dead, were it not that from time to time we could see that one of these holds a child pressed down among the fluttering banners of its misery.

Watching the beggars and their despair, in this civilisation that was made safe by war, the giant from the continent of darkness wrote: "A child, just dropt from its dam, may be supported by her milk for a solar year with little other nourishment . . . which the mother may get . . . or the value in scraps, by her lawful occupation of begging. . . . A young healthy child well nursed is at a year old a most delicious, nourishing, and wholesome food. . . . I do therefore humbly offer it to the public consideration, that of the hundred and twenty thousand children (of beggars) twenty thousand may be reserved for breed, whereof only one fourth part to be males, which is more than we allow to sheep, black cattle or swine. . . . That the remaining hundred thousand may at a year old be offered in sale to the persons of quality and fortune, through the kingdom, always advising the mother to let them suck plentifully in the last month, so as to render them plump and fit for a good table. . . . I have already computed the charge of nursing a beggar's child . . . to be about ten shillings per annum, rags included, and I believe no gentleman would refuse to give ten shillings for a good fat child."

Rag castle after rag castle, the world of beggars was swept along, and night fell upon the two nations who alone inhabit the earth, the rich and the poor.

E. S., *I Live Under a Black Sun.*

III

Tom o' Bedlam

From the hagg and hungrie goblin
That into ragges would rend ye,
And the spirit that stands by the naked man
In the Book of Moones defend ye!
That of your five sounde sences
You never be forsaken,
Nor wander from yourselves with Tom
Abroad to begg your bacon.

While I doe sing " Any foode, any feeding,
Feedinge, drinke or clothing,"
Come dame or maid, be not afraid,
Poor Tom will injure nothing.

Of thirty bare yeares have I
Twice twenty bin enragèd
And of forty bin three tymes fifteene
In durance soundlie cagèd
On the lordlie loftes of Bedlam
With stubble softe and dainty,

Braue braceletts strong, sweet whips
ding-dong,
With wholsome hunger plenty.
And now I sing, etc.

With a thought I tooke for Maudlin
And a cruse of cockle pottage,
With a thing thus tall, skie blesse you all,
I befell into this dotage.
I slept not since the Conquest,
Till then I never wakèd
Till the roguish boy of loue where I lay
Mee found and stript mee naked.
And now I sing, etc.

When I short have shorne my sowre face
And swigg'd my horny barrel
In an oaken inne, I pound my skin
As a suite of guilt apparell.
The moon's my constant Mistrisse
And the lowlie owle my morrowe,
The flaming Drake and the Nightcrowe make
Mee musicke to my sorrowe.
While I doe sing, etc.

The palsie plagues my pulses
When I prigg your pigs or pullen,
Your culvers take, or matchles make
Your chanticleare or sullen;
When I want prouant with Humfrie
I sup, and when benighted
I repose in Powles with waking soules
Yet nevere am affrighted.
But I doe sing, etc.

I knowe more than Apollo,
For oft when hee ly's sleeping
I see the starres at bloudie warres
In the wounded welkin weeping,
The moone embrace her shepheard
And the quene of Love her warryor,
While the first doth horne the star of morne
And the next the heavenly Farrier.

While I doe sing, etc.

The Gipsie snap and Pedro
Are none of Tom's comradoes.
The punk I skorne and the cut-purse sworn
And the roaring boyes bravadoe.
The meeke, the white, the gentle,
Me handle, touch and spare not;
But those that crosse Tom Rynosseros
Doe what the panther dare not.

Although I sing, etc.

With an host of furious fancies
Whereof I am commander,
With a burning speare, and a horse of aire,
To the wildernesse I wander.
By a knight of ghostes and shadowes
I summon'd am to tourney
Ten leagues beyond the wide world's end,
Mee thinkes it is noe journey.

Yet will I sing, etc.

ANON.

IV

The Chimney Sweeper — I

When my mother died I was very young,
And my father sold me while yet my tongue
Could scarcely cry " 'Weep ! 'Weep ! 'Weep ! 'Weep ! "
So your chimneys I sweep, & in soot I sleep.

There's little Tom Dacre, who cried when his head,
That curl'd like a lamb's back, was shav'd : so I said
" Hush, Tom ! never mind it, for when your head's bare
You know that the soot cannot spoil your white hair."

And so he was quiet, & that very night,
As Tom was sleeping, he had such a sight !
That thousands of sweepers, Dick, Joe, Ned, and Jack,
Were all of them lock'd up in coffins of black.

And by came an Angel who had a bright key,
And he open'd the coffins & set them all free ;
Then down a green plain leaping, laughing, they run,
And wash in a river, and shine in the Sun.

Then naked & white, all their bags left behind,
They rise upon clouds and sport in the wind ;
And the Angel told Tom, if he'd be a good boy,
He'd have God for his father, & never want joy.

And so Tom awoke ; and we rose in the dark,
And got with our bags & our brushes to work,
Tho' the morning was cold, Tom was happy & warm ;
So if all do their duty they need not fear harm.

William Blake.

V

The Chimney Sweeper — II

A little black thing among the snow
Crying " 'Weep ! 'Weep ! " in notes of woe !
" Where are thy father and mother, say ? "
" They are both gone up to the church to pray.

" Because I was happy upon the heath,
And smil'd among the winter's snow,
They clothed me in the clothes of death,
And taught me to sing the notes of woe.

" And because I am happy & dance & sing,
They think they have done me no injury,
And are gone to praise God & his Priest & King,
Who make up a heaven of our misery."

WILLIAM BLAKE.

VI

Hot Cake

Winter has come, fierce is the cold ;
In the sharp morning air new-risen we meet.
Rheum freezes in the nose,
Frost hangs about the chin.
For hollow bellies, for chattering teeth
and shivering knees
What better than hot cake ?
Soft as the down of spring,
Whiter than autumn floss.
Dense and swift the steam
Rises, swells and spreads.

Fragrance rises through the air,
Is scattered far and wide,
Steals down along the wind and wets
The covetous mouth of passer-by.
Servants and grooms
Cast sidelong glances, munch the
  empty air.
They lick their lips who serve;
While lines of envious lackeys by the wall
Stand dryly swallowing.

Part of a poem by Shu Hsi
(*c.* A.D. 265–306).
Translated from the Chinese by Arthur Waley.

VII

Of Flower-Shops in Winter

(Peking)

. . . .

These shops offer in mid-winter a synthesis of spring and early summer as the Chinese see it; to enter them is comparable to finding yourself in the fabulous flowery groves of a newly discovered continent, where all the flowers that grow in your own garden have been transmuted, through thousands of years of cultivation apart, into new forms, the flowers into new shapes, and invested with new and strange tones of colour, while within this small space has been condensed, also, the scent of whole orchards in an enchanted spring. . . . Here, indeed, the Chinese have indulged in their "peculiar propensity for dwarf and monstrous growth," as a former traveller[1] termed it. These little blossoming

[1] Robert Fortune.

trees (for the shops deal in plants more than in cut flowers), each crooked, bent branch in such perfect grotesque relationship to the next, so well balanced and inevitable that no other position for it would seem possible, might well have constituted the model for every Chinese decorative artist of the last twenty centuries. Furthermore, by no means the least pleasure to be derived from visiting these caged orchards was to watch the real Pekingese customers making their purchases. First, they would walk round the shop, examining all its contents, apples and quinces, peaches and cherries with their heads in little rosy clouds or bowed under a load of snow, orange-trees, bearing at the same time their blossoms and their fruit, some of these glowing like lamps, others green-bronze and nestling hidden in their glossy foliage, and little formal bushes of button roses, wistaria plants, about two or three feet high, coiled and serpentine, their drooping fragile clusters the colour of storm-clouds or an etiolate white. Having fixed his heart upon one particular example, the prospective buyer would then peer down at it for ten minutes at a time from every angle, appraising after this standard and his own experience its various faults and perfections, haggling inimitably over the price demanded — which seldom, even for Europeans, ranged up to more than four or five shillings — and pointing out to the blandly unconvinced shopkeeper a blemish, here, upon a petal, or a possible failure of line, there, in a twig.

It was a lengthy performance: but then it must be remembered that, by the custom of ages, the Chinese esthetic has been applied to flowers as much as paintings or sculptures, and that the cultivation of these winter trees constitutes an art, and a very ancient one. By the employment of this code, in addition to the very important question of symmetry, no plant and no single blossom can be allowed to belong to the category of the beautiful if it presents an ugly, or even an untidy, appearance at any stage of its development; however lovely it may be in flower, it is admired proportionately to its state of perfection in every season of the year, in bud, or when the petals are falling, or when the tree is bare, as much as in full bloom. Never must it look dishevelled or miserable. And for his own self-respect, it is necessary for the customer to bear all these points in mind before deciding which plant to buy.

According to Lich'en,[1] they are called "Hall-Flowers" in Peking, because, being a favourite present for the New Year, they stood in the hall of nearly every house there at the time of that festival. Peonies, plum blossom and red-peach blossom, jasmine, begonia and lilac were all for sale at that season (January and February), being reared in hot-houses by methods introduced into China during the Han Dynasty.

OSBERT SITWELL, *Escape with Me!*

[1] See Tun Lich'en's *Annual Customs and Festivals in Peking.*

On the Death of Flowers

It is opposed to all true philosophy to say that flowers lack their own eternity. They may perish and die here; but they will reappear in the restitution of all things. Nothing has been created out of the great Mystery which will not inhabit a form beyond the aether.

PARACELSUS. Book II.

Longing in Winter

Live they not against nature that in winter long for a Rose, and by the nourishment of warm waters, and the first change of heat in winter time, cause a lily, a spring flower, to bloom? Live they not against nature, that plant orchards on their highest towers, that have whole forests shaking upon the tops and turrets of their houses, spreading their roots in such places where it should suffice them that the tops of their branches should touch?

SENECA. Epistle 22.
Translated by Thomas Lodge.

The Flowering Flame

TSUNEYO. How cold it is! And as the night passes, each hour the frost grows keener. If I had but fuel to light a fire with, that you might sit by it and warm yourself! Ah! I have thought of something. I have some dwarf trees. I will cut them down and make a fire of them.

PRIEST. Have you indeed dwarf trees?

TSUNEYO. Yes, when I was in the World I had a fine show of them; but when my trouble came I had no more heart for tree-fancying, and gave them away. But three of them I kept—plum, cherry and pine. Look, there they are, covered with snow. They are precious to me; yet for this night's entertainment, I will gladly set light to them.

. . . .

[*Tsuneyo goes and stands by the dwarf trees. Then he brushed the snow from off them, and when he looked:*

"I cannot, cannot," he cried, "O beautiful trees,
Must I begin?
You, plum-tree, among bare boughs blossoming
Hard by the window, still on northward face
Snow-sealed, yet first to scent
Cold air with flowers, earliest of Spring;
You first shall fall.
You by whose boughs on mountain hedge entwined
Dull country folk have paused and caught their breath,
Hewn down for firewood. Little had I thought
My hand so pitiless!"

[*He cuts down the plum-tree.*

"You cherry (for each Spring your blossom comes
Behind the rest), I thought a lonely tree
And reared you tenderly, but now
I, *I* am lonely left, and you, cut down,
Shall flower but with flame."

From Hachi No Ki, by Seami.
Translated by Arthur Waley. *Nō Plays of Japan.*

BY THE FIRE

. . . where with a sweet and velvet lip
The snapdragons within the fire
Of their red summer never tire.

E. S.

I

To Larr

No more shall I, since I am driven hence,
Devote to thee my graines of Frankinsense :
No more shall I from mantle-trees hang downe
To honour thee, my little Parsly crowne :
No more shall I (I feare me) to thee bring
My chives of Garlick for an offering :
No more shall I, from henceforth, heare a quire
Of merry Crickets by my Country fire.
Go where I will, thou luckie Larr, stay here
Warme by a glitt'ring chimnie all the yeare.

ROBERT HERRICK.

II

Winter Night

This evening, Devotion to Circeto of the tall mirrors, fat as a fish and glowing like the ten months of the red night, (her heart is of amber and musk) — for my one prayer, mute as these regions of night.

Devotion. ARTHUR RIMBAUD.
Translated by Helen Rootham.

III

Upon Julia's Voice

So smooth, so sweet, so silv'ry is thy voice,
As, could they hear, the Damned would make no noise,
But listen to thee, (walking in thy chamber)
Melting melodious words to Lutes of Amber.

ROBERT HERRICK.

IV

Young Woman

And softe he cougheth with a semysoun :
What do ye, hony-comb, sweete Alisoun,
My faire bryd, my sweete cynamone.

GEOFFREY CHAUCER.

V

Old Woman

And in New Place a slack dishonoured body that once was comely, as sweet, as fresh, as cinnamon, now her leaves falling, all, bare, frighted of the narrow grave and unforgiven.

JAMES JOYCE, *Ulysses*.

VI

Of Friendship

. . . it is not ill that you entertain brave friendships and worthy societies : it were well if you could *love*, and if you could *benefit*, all mankinde : for I conceive that is the sum of all friendships.

I confess this is not to be expected of us in this world; but as all our graces here are but imperfect, that is, at the best they are but tendencies to glory, so our friendships are imperfect too, and but beginnings of a celestial friendship, by which we shall love every one as much as they can be loved.

. . . .

. . . but yet, *as any man hath anything of the good . . . so he can have and must have his share of friendship.* For thus the Sun is the eye of all the World; and he is indifferent to the Negro, or the cold Russian, to them that dwell under the line, and them that stand near the tropics, the scalded Indian or the poor boy that shakes at the foot of the Riphean hills, but the fluxures of the heaven and the earth, the conveniency of aboad, and the approaches to the North or South respectively change the emanations of his beams; not that they do not pass alwayes from him, but that they are not equally received below but by periods and changes, by little inlets and reflections, they receive what they can; and some have only a dark day and a long night from him, snowes and white cattel, a miserable life, and a perpetual harvest of catarrhes and consumptions, apoplexies and dead-palsies; but some have splendid fires, and aromatick spices, rich wines, and well digested fruits, great wit and great courage; because they dwell in his eye, and look in his face, and are the Courtiers of the Sun, and wait upon him in his Chambers of the East; just so is it in friendships: some are worthy, and some are necessary; some dwell hard by and are fitted for converse; Nature joyns some to us, and Religion combines us with others.

JEREMY TAYLOR, *Discourse of Friendship*, 1657.

VII

Of the Seasons of His Mercies

. . . God hath made no decree to distinguish the seasons of his mercies ; In paradise, the fruits were ripe, the first minute, and in heaven it is alwaies Autumne, his mercies are ever in their maturity. We ask *panem quotidianum*, our daily bread, and God never sayes you should have come yesterday, he never sayes you must againe to-morrow, but *to-day*, *if you will heare his voice*, to-day he will heare you. If some King of the earth have so large an extent of Dominion, in North, and South, as that he hath Winter and Summer together in his Dominions, so large an extent East and West, as that he hath day and night together in his Dominions, much more hath God mercy and judgement together : He brought light out of darknesse, not out of a lesser light ; he can bring thy Summer out of Winter, though thou have no Spring ; though in the wayes of fortune, or understanding, or conscience, thou have been benighted till now, wintred and frozen, clouded and eclypsed, damped and benummed, smothered and stupified till now, now God comes to thee, not as in the dawning of the day, not as in the bud of the spring, but as the Sun at noon to illustrate all shadowes, as the sheaves in harvest, to fill all penuries, all occasions invite his mercies, and all times are his seasons.

JOHN DONNE, Sermon II.
Preached at St. Paul's, upon Christmas Day,
in the evening, 1624.

THE COMPANIONS BY THE FIRE

I

Plant and Animal

An animal is a flower without a stem.

. . . .

The plant is an animal retarded by the darkness ; the animal is a plant blossoming directly through the light, and devoid of root.

. . . .

If the Animal is the floral vesicle living from or by itself, it can no longer be fettered like the plant, between the elements ; it must be nominally free from the chains of darkness, and thus from the earth. . . . No animal co-exists in two elements like the plant, but it has all elements in itself, as the flower includes all vegetable parts. . . .

. . . .

Animals are entire heavenly bodies, satellites or moons, which circulate independently about the earth. All plants, on the contrary, taken together, are only equivalent to one heavenly body. An animal is an infinity of plants.

LORENZ OKEN, *Elements of Physiophilosophy.*

II

The Cat

I will consider my Cat Jeoffry.
For he is the servant of the Living God, duly and daily
serving him.

For at the first glance of the glory of God in the East
he worships in his way.
For this is done by wreathing his body seven times
round with elegant quickness.
For then he leaps up to catch the musk, which is the
blessing of God upon his prayer.
For he rolls upon prank to work it in.
For having done duty and received blessing he begins to
consider himself.
For this he performs in ten degrees.
For first he looks at his fore-paws to see if they are clean.
For secondly he kicks up behind to clear away there.
For thirdly he works it upon stretch with the fore-paws
extended.
For fourthly he sharpens his paws by wood.
For fifthly he washes himself.
For sixthly he rolls upon wash.
For Seventhly he fleas himself, that he may not be
interrupted upon the beat.

. . . .

For Ninthly he looks up for instructions.
For Tenthly he goes in quest of food.
For having consider'd God and himself he will consider
his neighbour:
If he meets another cat he will kiss her in kindness;
For when he takes his prey he plays with it to give it
(a) chance:
For one mouse in seven escapes by his dallying.
For when his day's work is done his business more
properly begins.
For he keeps the Lord's watch in the night against the
adversary.
For he counteracts the powers of darkness by his
electrical skin and glaring eyes.

For he counteracts the Devil, who is death, by brisking
about the life.
For in his morning orisons he loves the sun and the sun
loves him.
For he is of the tribe of Tiger.
For the Cherub Cat is a term of the Angel Tiger.
For he has the subtlety and hissing of a serpent, which
in goodness he suppresses.
For he will not do destruction, if he is well-fed, neither
will he spit without provocation.
For he purrs in thankfulness, when God tells him he's
a good Cat.
For he is an instrument for the children to learn bene-
volence upon;
For every house is incompleat without him and a bless-
ing is lacking in the spirit.

. . . .

For he is the cleanest in the use of his fore-paws of any
quadruped.
For the dexterity of his defence is an instance of the love
of God to him exceedingly.
For he is the quickest to his mark of any creature.
For he is tenacious of his point.
For he is a mixture of gravity and waggery.
For he knows that God is his Saviour.
For there is nothing sweeter than his peace when at rest.
For there is nothing brisker than his life when in motion.

. . . .

For the divine spirit comes about his body to sustain it
in complete cat.
For his tongue is exceedingly pure so that it has in
purity what it wants in musick.

. . . .

For by stroking of him I have found out electricity.
For I perceived God's light about him both wax and fire.

. . . .

For God has blessed him in the variety of his movements.
For, tho' he cannot fly, he is an excellent clamberer.

. . . .

CHRISTOPHER SMART, *Rejoice with the Lamb.*

SUMMER RECIPES TO BE USED IN WINTER

I

How to draw the True Spirit of Roses

Macerate the rose either in water, or in his own juyce, adding thereto, being temperately warm, in convenient proportion, either of yest or ferment, leave them so a few days in fermentation, till they have gotten a strong and heady smel, and beginning to incline towards vinegar. Then distil them in Balneo, in glass bodies — (bottles? — print indistinct), luted to their helms, and draw so long as you find any scent of the rose to come; then redistill; or rectifie the same so often till you have purchased a perfect spirit. Also if you ferment the juyce of Roses onely, without any leaves mixed therein, you may draw an excellent spirit from the same; or if you keep the juyce of damask roses onely in close vessels well seasoned with the rose, it will yeeld a delicate spirit, after it hath wrought itself to a sufficient head by the inward rotation or circulation of nature. . . .

The last way, and the best way of all other that I know, is, by an outward fire to stir up the moist and inward fire of nature, till the same be grown to the subtilnesse of a rose wine, and when you have once brought it to a wine, then every Apothecary and ordinary practitioner in this art will easily divide his spirit from him; but they all will stagger in the first digestion; and though they should either reel or fall, I may not lend them my helping hand, otherwise than I have done already, unless I were assured that they were of the number of Hermes' sons, and not begotten by some base Alchemist.

SIR HUGH PLATT, *Jewel-house of Art and Nature*, 1594.

II

Rose-water and Rose-vinegar of the Colour of the Rose: and Violet Vinegar

. . . If you would make your Rose-water and Rose-vinegar, of a Rubie colour, then make choyce of the crimson velvet coloured leaves, clipping away the white with a paire of sheers; and being thorow dryed, put a good large handfull of them into a pint of Damask or red Rose-water: stop your glasse well and set it in the sunne, till you see that the leaves have lost their colour: or, for more expedition, you may perform this work in *balneo* in a few hours; and when you take out the old leaves you may put in fresh, till you find the colour to please you. Keepe this Rose-water in the glasses very well stopt, and the fuller, the better. What I have said of Rose-water, the same may, also, be intended of Rose-vinegar, (and violet . . .) but the whiter vinegar you chuse for the purpose, the colour thereof will be the better.

Ibid.

III

To make Sirrup of Violets

First gather a great quantity of violet flowers and pick them clean from the stalkes and set them on the fire and put to them so much rose-water as you think good. Then let them boil all together untill the colour be forth of them. Then take them off the fire and strain them through a fine cloth, and put so much sugar to them as you thinke good, then set it againe to the fire until it be somewhat thick and put it into a violet glasse.

The Good Housewife's Jewell, 1585.

IV

To make Gilliflower Wine

Take two ounces of dryed Gilliflowers, and put them into a bottle of Sack, and beat three ounces of Sugar candy, and fine Sugar, and grinde some Ambergreese, and put it in the bottle and shake it oft, then run it through a jelly bag. And give it for a great Cordiall.

The Queen's Closet Opened,
by W. M., Cook to Queen Henrietta Maria, 1665.

V

To raise a Rainbow

. . . yf . . . (a) serpent be burned and the ashes of ii put in ye fyre, anone shall there be a raine bowe with an horible thunder.

The Boke of the Secrets of Albertus Magnus.

For a Solemn Music

It will ask more than the work of twenty licensers to examine all the lutes, the violins, and the guitars in every house: they must not be suffered to prattle as they do, but must be licensed what they may say. And who shall silence all the airs and madrigals that whisper softness in chambers?

JOHN MILTON, *Areopagitica.*

THE THREE PLEASANT GHOSTS

I

To his Honoured Kinsman, Sir William Soame

I can but name thee, and methinkes I call
All that have been, or are Canonicall
For love and bountie, to come neare, and see
Their many vertues volumn'd up in thee ;
In thee Brave Man ! Whose incorrupted fame
Casts forth a light like to a Virgin flame ;
And as it shines, it throwes a scent about,
As when a Rain-bow in perfumes goes out.
So vanish hence, but leave a name, as sweet
As Benjamin and Storax, when they meet.

ROBERT HERRICK.

II

An Apparition

Anno 1670, not far from Cyrencester, was an Apparition. Being demanded whether a good Spirit or a Bad ? returned no answer, but disappeared with a curious Perfume, and a most melodious twang. Mr. W. Lillie believes it was a Fairy.

JOHN AUBREY, *Miscellanies.*

III

The Laird Bocconi

The Lord Middleton had a great Friendship with the Laird Bocconi, and they had made an agreement, that the first of them that died, should appear to the other in Extremity. The Lord Middleton was taken prisoner at Worcester Fight, and was Prisoner in the Tower under three Locks. Lying in his bed, pensive, Bocconi appeared to him; my Lord Middleton asked him if he were dead or alive? He said Dead, and told him that he was a Ghost: and told him that within three Days he should escape, and he did so in his Wife's Clothes. When he had done his Message, he gave a Frisk, and said

> "Givenni, Givanni 'tis very strange
> In the world to see so sudden a change,"

and then gathered up and vanished.

JOHN AUBREY, *Miscellanies.*

The Spirits on the Stairs

. . . In those darke Elizabethan times, astrologer, mathematician, and conjurer were accounted the same things; (Thomas Allen's) . . . servitor, to impose on freshmen and simple people, would tell them that sometimes he should meet the spirits coming up his stairs like bees.

JOHN AUBREY, *Brief Lives.*

The Courteous Spirits

I do think that many mysteries ascribed to our inventions, have been the courteous revelations of Spirits; (for these noble essences in Heaven bear a friendly regard unto their fellow Natures on Earth).

SIR THOMAS BROWNE, *Religio Medici.*

A Digression of the Nature of Spirits, Bad Angels, or Devils

. . . Bodine . . . will have these *animae separatae*, (abstract souls) genii, spirits, devils . . . to be of some shape, and that absolutely round, like sun and moon, because that is the most perfect form, *quae nihil habet asperitatis, nihil angulis incisum, nihil anfractibus involutum, nihil eminens, sed inter corpora perfecta est perfectissimum* (which has no rough edges, no corners, no twists, no projections, but is the most perfect of shapes). . . .

That they can assume other aerial bodies; all manner of shapes at their pleasures, appear in what likeness they will themselves, that they are most swift in motion, can pass many miles in an instant, and so likewise transform bodies of others into what shape they please, and with admirable celerity remove them from place to place; . . . that they can represent castles in the air, palaces, armies, spectrums, prodigies, and such strange objects to mortal men's eyes, cause smells, savours, etc., deceive all the senses: most writers of this subject credibly believe; and that they can foretell future events, and do many strange miracles.

. . . .

And Leo Suavius, a Frenchman . . . out of some Platonists, will have the air to be full of them as snow falling in the skies, and that they may be seen, and withal sets down the means how men may see them.

. . . .

Cardan, in his *Hyperchen*, out of the doctrine of Stoics, will have some of these genii (for so he calls them) to be desirous of men's company, very affable and familiar with them, as dogs are.

. . . .

Terrestrial devils are those lares, genii, fauns, satyrs, wood-nymphs, foliots, fairies, Robin Goodfellows, trolli (trolls) etc. which as they are most conversant with men, so they do them most harm. Some think it was they alone that kept the heathen people in awe of old, and had so many idols and temples erected to them. . . . Some put our fairies into this rank, which have been in former times adored with much superstition, with sweeping their houses, and setting a pail of clean water, good victuals and the like, and then they shall not be pinched, but find money in their shoes, and be fortunate in their enterprises. These are they that dance on heaths and greens, as Lavater thinks with Trithemius, and as Olaus Magnus adds, leave that green circle, which we commonly find in plain fields, which others hold to proceed from a meteor falling, or some accidental rankness of the ground, so Nature sports herself; they are sometimes seen by old women and children.

. . . .

Paracelsus reckons up many places in Germany, where they do usually walk in little coats, some two feet long. A bigger kind there is of them called with us hobgoblins, and Robin Goodfellows, that would in these superstitious times grind corn for a mess of milk, cut wood, or do any manner of drudgery work. . . . Another sort of these there are, which frequent forlorn houses, which Italians call foliots, most part innocuous,—Cardan holds. They will make strange noises in the night, howl sometimes pitifully, and then laugh again, cause great flame and sudden lights.

ROBERT BURTON, *The Anatomy of Melancholy.*

The Drum: the Narrative of the Drummer of Tedworth

In his tall senatorial
Black and manorial
House where decoy-duck
Dust doth clack —
Clatter and quack
To a shadow black —
Said the musty Justice Mompesson:
"What is that dark stark beating drum
That we hear rolling like the sea?"

" It is a beggar with a pass
Signed by you." " I signed not one."
They took the ragged drum that we
Once heard rolling like the sea ;
In the house of the Justice it must lie
And usher in Eternity.

. . . .

Is it black night ?
Black as Hecate howls a star
Wolfishly, and whined
The wind from very far.

In the pomp of the Mompesson house is one
Candle that lolls like the midnight sun,
Or the coral comb of a cock ; . . . it rocks. . . .
Only the goatish snow's locks
Watch the candles lit by fright
One by one through the black night.

Through the kitchen there runs a hare —
Whinnying, whines like grass, the air ;
It passes ; now is standing there
A lovely lady . . . see her eyes —
Black angels in a heavenly place,
Her shady locks and her dangerous grace.

" I thought I saw the wicked old witch in
The richest gallipot in the kitchen ! "
A lolloping galloping candle confesses.
" Outside in the passage are wildernesses
Of darkness rustling like witches' dresses."

Out go the candles one by one,
Hearing the beating of a drum !

What is the march we hear groan
As the hoofèd sound of a drum marched on
With a pang like darkness, with a clang
Blacker than an orang-outang?
" Heliogabalus is alone, —
Only his bones to play upon."

The mocking money in the pockets
Then turned black . . . now caws
The fire . . . outside, one scratched the door
As with iron claws, —

Scratching under the children's bed
And up the trembling stairs . . . " Long dead "
Moaned the water black as crape.
Over the snow the wintry moon
Limp as henbane, or herb paris,
Spotted the bare trees; and soon

Whinnying, neighed the maned blue wind,
Turning the burning milk to snow:
Whining it shied down the corridor —
Over the floor I heard it go
Where the drum rolls up the stair, nor tarries.

E. S.

OF THE FAIRIES

I

Queene Mab

MERCUTIO. O! then, I see Queene Mab hath beene with you.

BENVOLIO. Queene Mab? What's she?

MERCUTIO. She is the Fairies Midwife, and she comes
In shape no bigger than an Agat-stone
On the forefinger of an Alderman,
Drawne with a teame of little Atomies,
Athwart men's noses as they lie asleepe;
Her Waggon Spokes made of long spinners' legs;
The Cover, of the wings of Grasshoppers;
The Traces, of the smallest Spider's web;
The Collars, of the Moonshine's watery Beames;
Her Whip, of Cricket's bone; the Lash, of filme,
Her Waggoner, a small grey-coated Gnat,
Not halfe as bigge as a round little Worme
Prick'd from the lazy finger of a Maid;
Her Chariot is an empty Hazel nut
Made by the joyner Squirrel or old Grub,
Time out o' mind the Fairies' Coach-makers.
And in this state she gallops night by night
Through Lovers' braines, and then they dreame of love;
O'er Courtiers' knees, that dreame on Court'sies straight;
O'er Lawyers' fingers, who straight dreame on fees;
O'er Ladies' lips, who straight on kisses dreame;
Which oft the angry Mab with blisters plagues,
Because their breaths with sweetmeats tainted are.

Sometimes she gallops o'er a Courtier's nose,
And then dreames he of smelling out a suit;
And sometimes comes she with a Tithe-pig's tail,
Tickling a Parson's nose as 'a lies asleepe,
Then dreames he of another Benefice;
Sometimes she driveth o'er a Souldier's necke,
And then dreames he of cutting Forraine throats,
Of Breaches, Ambuscadoes, Spanish Blades,
Of Healths five Fadome deepe; and then anon
Drums at his eare, at which he starts and wakes;
And, being thus frighted, sweares a prayer or two,
And sleepes againe. This is that very Mab
That plats the manes of Horses in the night,
And bakes the Elf-locks in foul sluttish haires
Which, once entangled, much misfortune bodes;
This is the hag, when maids lie on their backs,
That presses them, and learns them first to beare,
Making them women of good carriage:
This she——

ROMEO. Peace, peace! Mercutio, peace!
Thou talk'st of nothing.

MERCUTIO. True, I talke of dreames:
Which are the children of an idle braine,
Begot of nothing but vaine phantasie;
Which is as thin of substance as the ayre,
And more inconstant than the wind, who wooes
Even now the frozen bosome of the North,
And, being anger'd, puffes away from thence,
Turning his face to the dew-dropping South.

. . . .

WILLIAM SHAKESPEARE,
Romeo and Juliet, Act I, Scene IV.

II

A Song of Robin Goodfellow

Now the hungrie lyon rores
 And the wolfe behowls the moon ;
Whilst the heavy ploughman snores,
 All with wearie task fore-done.
Now the wasted brands doe glow,
 While the screech-owl, screeching loud,
Puts the wretch that lyes in woe
 In remembrance of a shroud.
Now it is the time of night
 That the graves, all gaping wide,
Every one lets forth his sprite,
 In the church-way paths to glide :
And we Fairies, that doe runne
 By the triple Hecate's teame,
From the presence of the Sunne,
 Following darknesse like a dreame,
Now are frollicke ; not a Mouse
Shall disturb this hallowed house :
I am sent with broome before
To sweep the dust behinde the doore.

WILLIAM SHAKESPEARE,
A Midsommer Night's Dreame, Act V, Scene II.

III

The Jackman's Song

The faery beame upon you,
The starres to glister on you ;
 A Moone of light,
 In the Noone of night,

Till the Fire Drake hath o'er gone you.
The Wheele of Fortune guide you,
The Boy with the Bow beside you,
    Runne aye in the way,
    Till the Bird of Day
And the luckyer lot betide you.

BEN JONSON.

Of the Absence of Glo-wormes

The *Nature* of the Glo-worme is hitherto not well observed. Thus much we see; that they breed chiefly in the *Hottest Moneths* of Summer. And that they breed . . . in *Bushes* and *Hedges*. Whereby it may be conceived, that the Spirit of them is very fine, and not to be refined, but by *Summer Heate*: and againe, that by reason of the Finenesse, it doth easily exhale. In *Italy*, and the *Hotter Countries*, there is a Flie they call *Lucciole*, that shineth as the Glo-worme doth; and it may be is the *Flying Glo-worme*. But that Flie is chiefly upon *Fens*, and *Marrishes*. But yet the two former *Observations* hold; for they are not seene, but in the *Heat* of Summer; and Sedge, or other *Greene* of the Fens, give as good Shade as Bushes. It may be the *Glo-wormes* of the *Cold Countries* ripen not so far as to be *Winged*.

FRANCIS BACON, *Naturall History*. Century VIII.

Night—I

When one feels oneself sleeping alone, utterly divided from all call or hearing of friends, doors open that should be shut, or unlocked that should be triply secured, the very walls gone, barriers swallowed up by unknown abysses, nothing around one but frail curtains, and a world of illimitable night, whisperings at a distance, correspondence going on between darkness and darkness, like one deep calling to another, and the dreamer's own heart the centre from which the whole network of this unimaginable chaos radiates, by means of which the blank *privations* of silence and darkness become powers the most *positive* and awful.

THOMAS DE QUINCEY, *The Avenger*.

The Apparition

. . . . . .

. . . All rose before the agèd Apparition
His snowy beard that streams like lambent flames down
his wide breast
Wetting with tears, & his white garments cast a wintry
light.
Then, as arm'd clouds arise terrific round the northern
drum,
The world is silent at the flapping of the folding banners;
So still terrors rent the house. . . .

WILLIAM BLAKE, Appendix to *America*.

Night — II

Still the faint harps & silver voices calm the weary
couch,
But from the caves of deepest night, ascending in
clouds of mist,
The winter spread his wide black wings across from
pole to pole:
Grim frost beneath & terrible snow, link'd in a marriage
chain,
Began a dismal dance. The winds around on pointed
rocks
Settled like bats innumerable, ready to fly abroad.

WILLIAM BLAKE, *The Four Zoas*. Night V.

The Terrible Stars

These blazing starres that the Greekes call *Cometas*, our Romanes *Crinitas*, dreadfull to be seene, with bloudie haires, and all over rough and shagged in the top like the bush of haire upon the head. The same Greekes call those starres *Pogonias*, which from the nether part have a maine hanging downe, in fashion of a long beard. As for those called *Acontiæ*, they brandish and shake like a speare or dart, signifying great swiftnesse. This was it, whereof Tiberius the Emperour wrote an excellent Poeme in his fift Consulship, the last that ever was seene to this day: the same, if they be shorter and sharpe pointed in the top, they use to call *Xiphiæ*; and of all other palest they be, and glitter like a sword, but without any raies or beames. . . .

. . . .

Lampadias is like to burning torches and *Hippeus* to horse maines, most swift in motion and turning round. There is also a white Comet with silver haires, so bright and shining, that hardly a man can endure to looke upon it, and in man's shape it sheweth the verie image of a God. Moreover, there be blazing starres that become all shaggie, compassed round with hairie fringe and a kind of maine. One heretofore appearing in the form of a main, changed into a speare, namely in the hundred and eight Olympias, and the 398 yeare from the foundation of Rome. Noted it hath ben, that the shortest time of their appearance is a seven night, and the longest eightie daies. Some of them move like the wandering planets: others are fixed fast, and stir not. All in manner are seene under the very North star called Charlemagne's Wain. . . . There are of them seene in winter season, and about the Antarticke South pole: but in that place without any beames. A terrible one likewise was seene of the people in Ethiopia and Egypt, which the King who raigned in that age, named Typhon. It resembled fire, and was plaited and twisted in maner of a wreath, grim and hideous to be looked on; and no more truly to be counted a starre, than some knot of fire.

Sometimes it falleth out, that the *Plannets* and other stars are bespread all over with haires. But a *Comet* lightly is never seen in the west part of the heaven. . . .

A fearefull starre for the most part this Comet is, and not easily expiated: as it appeared by the late civile troubles when *Octavius* was Consull: as also a second time by the intestine war of *Pompey* and *Cæsar*. And in our daies about the time that *Claudius Cæsar* was poysoned, and left the Empire to *Domitius Nero*, in the time of whose raigne and government, there was another in manner continually seene, and ever terrible. . . .

PLINY.
Translated by Philemon Holland.

Of a Death in Winter

I

. . . .

Manshape, that shone
Sheer off, disseveral, a star, / death blots black out;
nor mark
Is any of him at all so stark
But vastness blurs and time / beats level. Enough!
The Resurrection.
A heart's-clarion! Away grief's gasping, joyless days,
dejection.

Across my foundering deck shone
A beacon, an eternal beam. / Flesh fade, and mortal trash
Fall to the residuary worm ; / world's wildfare, leave but ash :
In a flash, at a trumpet crash,
I am all at once what Christ is, / since he was what I am, and
This Jack, joke, poor potsherd, / patch, matchwood, immortal diamond,
Is immortal diamond.

GERARD MANLEY HOPKINS. From *That Nature is a Heraclitean Fire and of the Comfort of the Resurrection.*

II

. . . .

The ravenous earth that now wooes her to be
Earth too, will be a Lemnia ; and the tree
That wraps that christall in a wooden Tombe
Shall be tooke up spruce, fill'd with diamond.

JOHN DONNE. From *Elegie : Death.*

Sonnet of Black Beauty

Black beauty, which above that common light,
Whose Power can no colours here renew,
But those which darkness can again subdue,
Do'st still remain unvary'd to the sight,

And like an object equal to the view,
Art neither chang'd with day, nor hid with night ;
When all these colours which the world call bright,
And which old Poetry doth so persue,

Are with the night so perished and gone,
    That of their being there remains no mark,
Thou still abidest so intirely one,
    That we may know thy blackness is a spark
Of light inaccessible, and alone
    Our darkness which can make us think it dark.

LORD HERBERT OF CHERBURY.

AT A TIME OF DARKNESS

I

Thou, Eternal Trinity, art my creator, and I am the work of Thy hands, and I know through Thy new creation which Thou hast given me in the Blood of Thy Son that Thou art enamoured of the beauty of Thy workmanship. Oh ! Abyss, Oh ! Eternal Godhead, Oh ! Sea Profound, What more couldst Thou give me than Thyself, Thou art the fire which ever burns, without being consumed ; Thou consumest in Thy heat all the soul's self-love ; Thou art the fire which takes away all cold ; with Thy light Thou dost illuminate me so that I may know all Thy truth ; Thou art that light above all light which illuminates supernaturally the eye of my intellect, clarifying the light of faith so abundantly and so perfectly that I may see that my soul is alive, and in this light receive Thee — the true light.

SAINT CATHERINE OF SIENA.

II

A Prayer for Those Who Weep for the World

The God of Tears ! What do these two words mean and what is this God? None other than the Holy Spirit. It is through Him that we are alive, and tears are the sign of his presence. . . . *Tears are so much the gift of the Holy Spirit that whenever they flow God must needs draw near*, since He said that He Himself would wipe away tears from off all faces. They are so precious that we are not permitted to shed them in vain.

Lord God! Grant me to weep when waking and when sleeping, to weep always as did Thy prophet. If my tears are not pure, change them into blood, and if that blood is worthless, let it become rivers of fire; but, no matter how, make me weep, since therein lies the means of blessedness, the infallible secret of drawing down the Comforter! Consider the infinite multitude of men who have wept since the beginning of time. I know well that many of their tears were in vain. There were tears of pride and tears of lust; there were tears of hate and of anger. But there were and there are always, the tears of that Suffering which Thou didst wed for love. Their abundance is as the Flood, and Thy Spirit moves upon the face of the waters as of old, when Thou hadst not yet created the world.

LÉON BLOY, a letter quoted in Albert Béguin's *Léon Bloy*.

III

Since we are taught from our earliest days that we were created in God's image, is it then so difficult simply to suppose . . . that there must be in the Impenetrable Essence *something corresponding to ourselves, without sin*, and that the grievous conspectus of human afflictions is but a dark reflex of the inexpressible conflagrations of Light?

LÉON BLOY, *Le Salut pour les Juifs*.

IV

The Divine Darkness

Trinity, which exceedeth all Being, Deity, and Goodness! Thou that instructeth Christians in Thy heavenly wisdom! Guide us to that topmost height of mystic love which exceedeth light and more than exceedeth knowledge, where the simple, absolute, and unchangeable mysteries of heavenly Truth lie hidden in the dazzling obscurity of the secret Silence, outshining all brilliance with the intensity of their darkness, and surcharging our blinded intellects with the utter impalpable and invisible fairness of glories which exceed all beauty! Such is my prayer; and thee, dear Timothy, I counsel that in the earnest exercise of mystical contemplation thou leave the senses and the activities of the intellect and all things that the senses of the intellect can perceive, and all things in this world of nothingness, or in that world of being. . . . For, by the unceasing and absolute renunciation of thyself and all things, thou shalt in pureness cast all things aside, and be released from all, and so shalt be led upwards to the Ray of that divine Darkness, which exceedeth all existence.

DIONYSIUS THE AREOPAGITE, *On the Divine Names and the Mystical Theology*. . .
Translated by C. E. Rolt.

Of Crystal and Icicles

As for the figure of Crystal (which is very strange, and forced Pliny to despair of resolution) it is for the most part hexagonal. It is a Minerall body in the difference of Stones, and reduced by some into that subdivision which comprehendeth gemms, transparent and resembling Glas or Ice, made of a lenrous percolation of earth, drawn from the most pure and limpid juice thereof, owing, unto the coldness of the earth some concurrence or coadjuvancy, but not immediate determination and efficiency, which are wrought by the hand of its concretive spirit, the seeds of petrification and Gorgon of itself. As sensible Philosophers conceive of the generation of Diamonds, Iris, Beryls. Not making them of frozen Icecles, or from such agreous and glaciable substances, condensing them by frosts into solidities, vainly to be expected even from Polary congelations: but from thin and finest earths, so well tempered and resolved, that transparency is not hindered. . . .

. . . .

SIR THOMAS BROWNE,
Enquiry into Vulgar and Common Errors.

The Hat given to the Poet by Li-Chien
(Died A.D. 821)

Long ago to a white-haired gentleman
You made the present of a black gauze hat.
The gauze hat still sits on my head;
But you already are gone to the Nether Springs.
The thing is old, but still fit to wear;
The man is gone and will never be seen again.
Out on the hills the moon is shining to-night
And the trees on your tomb are swayed by the autumn
wind.

PO CHÜ-I.
Translated from the Chinese by Arthur Waley.

Song

Urns and Odours, bring away!
Vapours, sighs, darken the day!

Our dole more deadlier looks than dying ;
    Balmes and gums, and heavie cheeres,
    Sacred vial fill'd with teares,
And clamours through the wild air flying !

Come, all sad and solemn shows
    That are quick-ey'd Pleasure's foes !
We convent nought else but woes :
We convent nought else but woes.

WILLIAM SHAKESPEARE ? JOHN FLETCHER ?
The Two Noble Kinsmen.

Wild Weather

(Act I, Scene I. The Temple of Isis)

Enter SERAPION, MYRIS, PRIESTS OF ISIS.

SERAPION. Portents and Prodigies are grown so frequent
That they have lost their Name. Our fruitfull Nile
Flow'd ere the wonted season, with a Torrent
That, the wild Deluge overtook the haste,
Ev'n of the Hinds that watch'd it : Men and Beasts
Were borne above the tops of Trees, that grew
On th' utmost margin of the Water-mark.
Then, with so swift an Ebb, the Floud drove backward
It slipt from underneath the Scaly Herd :
Here monstrous Phocae panted on the Shore ;
Forsaken Dolphins there, with their broad Tails
Lay lashing the departing Waves : Hard by 'em,
Sea-Horses floundring in the slimy Mud,
Toss'd up their heads, and dash'd the ooze about 'em.
MYRIS. Avert these Omens, Heav'n.

SERAPION. Last night, between the hours of Twelve and One,
On a lone Isle o' th' Temple, while I walk'd,
A whirlwind rose, that with a violent blast
Shook all the Dome : the Doors around me clapt,
The Iron Wicket that defends the Vault
Where the long Race of Ptolmies is lay'd
Burst open, and disclos'd the mighty Dead.
From out each Monument, in order plac'd,
An armed Ghost, start up : the Boy-King last
Rear'd his inglorious head : a peal of groans
Cry'd Egypt is no more. . . .

JOHN DRYDEN, *All for Love, or the World well Lost.*

Horus

Le dieu Kneph en tremblant ébranlait l'univers :
Isis, la mère, alors se lève sur sa couche,
Fit un geste de haine a son époux farouche,
Et l'ardeur d'autrefois brilla dans ses yeux verts.

" Le voyez-vous," dit-elle, " il meurt, ce vieux pervers,
Tous les frimas du monde ont passé par sa bouche,
Attachez son pied tors, éteignez son œil louche,
C'est le dieu des volcans et le roi des hivers !

" L'aigle a déjà passé, l'esprit nouvelle m'appelle,
J'ai revêtu pour lui la robe de Cybèle. . . .
C'est l'enfant bien-aimé d'Hermes et d'Osiris."

La déesse avait fui sur sa conque dorée,
La mer nous renvoyait son image, adorée.
Et les cieux rayonnaient sous l'écharpe d'Iris.

GÉRARD DE NERVAL.

Two Letters

I

" Why am I writing ? " he said in his letter. " I have lost you and there is no more to be said. But 'Though you be standing in the radiance of the Morning Sun, perchance one drop of dew may linger of those your sleeves once gathered in the shadowy garden-walks.' Did I but think you know how much it costs me to lose you I should derive some comfort." . . . The note containing this poem was attached to an ice-cold spray of bamboo, plucked from near the ground and carried with such care that it was still thickly coated with hoar-frost. The messenger was on this, as upon every other occasion, a person whose quality matched the elegance of the letter.

LADY MURASAKI, *Blue Trousers*.
Translated from the Japanese by Arthur Waley.

II

He trimmed his brush with the utmost care, and wrote on exquisite white paper : " No deep drift bars my path, but with their whirling these thin parched snowflakes have bewitched my dizzy brain." This he tied to a sprig of plum-blossom, and sending for one of his servants, bade him take it not across the garden, but by way of the western gallery.

LADY MURASAKI.
Translated from the Japanese by Arthur Waley.

After the Flood

As soon as the idea of the Flood had abated

A hare paused in the clover and shaking bell-flowers, and prayed to the rainbow through the spider's web.

What jewels gleamed in hiding — what flowers gazed about them.

In the dirty high-street sprang up the stalls, and boats were dragged towards the sea, staged above it as in old prints.

Blood washed the walls of Bluebeard's house, flowed in the slaughterhouses and in the circuses, where the windows grew livid beneath the seal of God. Blood and milk flowed.

Beavers built up their houses. Glasses of black coffee steamed in the little wine-shops.

In the great house of glass still streaming with water, children dressed in mourning looked at the marvellous pictures.

A door banged; and in the village market-place the child waved his arms to answer the vanes and the weather-cocks on all sides, under the glittering spatter.

Madame X set up a flat in the Alps, Masses and First Communions were celebrated at the hundred thousand altars of the cathedral.

Caravans set off. And the Hôtel-Splendide was built in the chaos of ice and night at the Pole.

Since then the moon has listened to the jackals whining in thyme-scented deserts—and eclogues in sabots grunting in the orchards. Then in the violet forest all a-burgeon, Eucharis called me, saying "It is spring."

Brim over, oh pool; foam, roll over the bridge, and cover the forests; sable cloths and organs, lightning and thunder, rise up and roll; waters and sorrows, rise and lift up the floods again.

Because since the floods fell, precious stones have so buried themselves, and flowers so opened in profusion, that it has become an untellable boredom! And the Queen, the Sorceress who kindles her glowing embers in the earthen pot, never will she consent to enlighten our ignorance.

ARTHUR RIMBAUD, *Les Illuminations*.
Translated by Helen Rootham.

THE END

PRINTED BY R. & R. CLARK, LTD., EDINBURGH